Bribery
and
Corruption

He forces us all to step beyond our dualism, to move past giving simple answers to complex questions, and to be humble in accepting that a brother or sister in another part of the world might make a decision that is different from the one we make in another context. I trust this book will be an inspiration, and a reason for hope, for all of those called by God to work in a setting where the path forward is neither easy nor clear.

Albert M. Erisman
Seattle Pacific University
Seattle, Washington, USA

The freedom for the Christian to choose his level of involvement in society is admirably treated. The conclusion that true moral transformation of society cannot be effected unless there is a spiritual revival is well made.

L. T. Jeyachandran
Former Executive Director
Ravi Zacharias International Ministries (Asia–Pacific)

It is certainly a worthy contribution to a very important challenge. It strikes me as both faithful to Scripture and practical/insightful for working Christians in the marketplace.... This careful essay on bribery and corruption makes a lot of sense to me. We need to get away from legalism and formalism and ask "what is the point here?" What are the values we are trying to protect? Corruption of justice and fairness?

David W. Gill
Ethixbiz

Hwa Yung

Bribery and Corruption

Biblical Reflections and Case Studies
for the Marketplace in Asia

Edited by Soo-Inn Tan

SECOND EDITION

Published by Graceworks Private Limited
22 Sin Ming Lane
#04–76 Midview City
Singapore 573969
E-mail: enquiries@graceworks.com.sg
Website: www.graceworks.com.sg

Designed by Atlas Associates Pte Ltd
82 Atrix Building
Lor 23 Geylang #05–13
Singapore 388409

ISBN: 978-981-11-6672-3

1 2 3 4 5 6 7 8 9 10 • 27 26 25 24 23 22 21 20 19 18

Contents

SECTION 3 — CASE STUDIES

REFERENCES

Introduction

"Ethics is like Mercedes Benz, Babe! Nice if you can afford it, but completely unnecessary!"

Brenda Starr Comics Strip

"Let your light so shine before men that they may see your good works and glorify your Father who is in heaven."

Matthew 5:16

The external pressures faced by Christians in the market-place in Asia are the same as those faced by Christians worldwide. They can be summed up by the words "money, sex and power". Christians often fail to take seriously the corrupting power of these three forces. In addition, their resources to cope with these forces are often inadequate. The inadequacies of the Christian's resources are three-fold. First, few of us have sufficient inner spiritual strength and pastoral support to deal with the relentless power of sin as manifested in the corporate world. Second, most evangelical and charismatic Christians have a basically dualistic worldview that separates faith and life, the religious from the secular. Such a "world-denying" theology, or "life-boat" ethics, has little or nothing positive to say in helping us come to terms with the problems of the world. The third problem is that even where help is available for us in the realm of ethics, most of these resources have been developed in the West, where the problems are manifested in quite different cultural or socioeconomic contexts. Therefore they may be irrelevant to our struggles in Asia, or, at best, speak inadequately to them.

This short book is one attempt to respond to the need to help Christians in Asia find a biblical response to the real pressures they face in the marketplace, which takes seriously both the Scriptures and the context in which Asian Christians function. In particular, I write from a Malaysian context since this is where I live and minister, and so it is the context I am most familiar with. However I believe the principles articulated here can also be applied to other parts of Asia and the two-thirds world.

Chapter one will look at the three main corrupting pressures faced by Christians in the marketplace, and our inadequate resources to counter them. Chapter two is a proposal for a biblical and theological framework for Christian ethical thinking in the Asian context. Chapter three will focus on the issue of bribery and corruption as a case study to illustrate the proposed approach.

* The first section in this book was originally a paper presented by Bishop Hwa Yung, entitled "Christian Ethical Thinking in the Malaysian Context".

SECTION 1 *BIBLICAL REFLECTIONS*

External Pressures and Inner Inadequacies

We begin by looking in detail at the external pressures faced by Christians in the world in general, and the corporate world in particular.

The External Pressures: "Money, Sex and Power"

The three-fold temptations of money, sex and power are the three themes that sum up neatly the pressures experienced in the corporate world today. One just has to look closely at any of the soap operas from the East or West to note the point. Indeed if we analyse them closely we will find that they bring into clear focus almost all the temptations of life. These pressures are experienced by all Christians, everywhere. The Christian monastic tradition has always understood this clearly. The three monastic vows of "poverty, chastity and obedience" are its direct responses to these three temptations. The same is true of the seventeenth-century Puritans' emphasis on industry, faithfulness, and order (Foster 1985, 4–12).

The most useful modern study of these three themes is Richard Foster's *Money, Sex and Power: The Spiritual*

Disciplines of Poverty, Chastity and Obedience (1985). I will briefly draw attention to some of the points he makes. Foster rightly notes that these three things are not evil in and of themselves. Each is a part of God's overall gift of life to us. But like all gifts from God, they can turn "bad" if misused or misappropriated. He therefore reminds that these are

> ...explosive themes that easily turn into "demons" that make of our lives one great sorrow.
>
> The demon in money is greed. Nothing can destroy human beings like the passion to possess. In *The Idiot*, Dostoevsky has one of his characters observe, "Every one is possessed with such a greed nowadays, they are all so overwhelmed by the idea of money that they seem to have gone mad."
>
> The demon in sex is lust. True sexuality leads to humanness, but lust leads to depersonalisation. Lust captivates rather than emancipates, devours rather than nourishes.
>
> The demon in power is pride. True power has as its aim to set people free, whereas pride is determined to dominate. True power enhances relationships; pride destroys them.
>
> The demons of greed, lust, and pride can be exorcised, but let me warn you that the exorcisms will not come easily or quickly (Foster 1985, 13).

Foster is right on target. The Bible's teachings on these themes are too well known to need repeating here. But I wonder whether we are sufficiently aware of their subtlety and destructive powers, or the relentless pressure they put on our fragile consciences and wills. In most churches there is a lack of teaching on these themes. Among Christians the tendency is to allow the world's values of riches and success to dominate life's major decisions like choices of careers and life partners. Moreover, some in the charismatic movement appear bent on promoting the "prosperity gospel" and its single-minded pursue of success and wealth. In general, many find it difficult to cope with the love and abuse of money, sex and power in everyday life. All these point to our blindness to the relentless and destructive power of these external pressures.

We need to ask: How many of our "successful" Christian leaders, both in church and in public life, have been able to maintain a life of integrity and simplicity that fully reflects the values of the Kingdom of God? How many have family lives that bear testing by the standards of the New Testament? How many have been able to live with a servant attitude, after the example of Christ, without succumbing to the corruption of power? And how much of our failures in these areas arise out of our naiveté towards the pressures upon us?

Our Inner Inadequacies

The above leads us to the question of whether we have sufficient inner spiritual and theological resources to cope with the pressures.

Inadequate spiritual resources

There are a number of areas where our inner spiritual resources are inadequate. The first is that not many of us recognise the full extent of the power of sin in our lives. It is not my purpose to discuss this comprehensively. Unfortunately, much of present-day popular Christian literature addresses this matter superficially at best.

However, good material on this can easily be found.[1] But the point that must be made is that sin is a pervasive corrupting power in our human nature and must be recognised as such. Reformed theologians speak of the pervasive corruption of sin in human lives as "total depravity", in the sense that nothing that we do can ever be totally good or pure. Martin Luther, the outstanding leader of the sixteenth-century Reformation, speaks of "The Bondage of the Will", the title of his most important book. Both emphases are consistent with biblical teaching (cf. Jer. 17:9; Mark 14:38b; Rom. 7:14–24).

Secondly, because of the grip sin has in our lives, we easily succumb to the inner corruption of the soul. In fact, our very being is already corrupted. We need to be freed from that corruption through the exercise of spiritual disciplines (Rom. 8:5–8) on the one hand and the power of the Holy Spirit (Rom. 8:9–13) on the other. But the world around us is far from being the holy space within

---

[1] To begin with, look at Foster (1985) on our weaknesses in relation to money, sex and power. Also refer to some good books on holiness like J. I. Packer's *A Passion for Holiness* (1992) and J. White's *The Pathway of Holiness* (1996); or see J. White's *Changing on the Inside* (1991) in which he discusses the dynamics of sin and repentance. For those who are interested in a powerful, modern, psychological study on the power of sin and evil (including self-deception) in human lives, see Scott Peck's *People of the Lie* (1983).

which these can take place. Indeed, it is, as our TV soap operas indicate, precisely the reverse of that — it is where the corrupting power of money, sex, and power is often experienced at its worst! But as we will see, because of the theological outlook of our churches, few struggling in this area find sufficient pastoral help to resist the further corruption of our souls.

A dualistic worldview

The second major area where our inner resources are inadequate encompasses the forming of a holistic understanding of the world. This is due to the fact that most of us have absorbed into our intellectual systems a basically Western theology. This theology is, as we shall see, fundamentally dualistic.

At the simplest level, this can be seen in the Platonic separation of the human person into the body, which belongs to the imperfect phenomenal world (i.e. the real world we live in), and the soul, which belongs to the perfect world (what Plato calls the world of Forms). Whereas the Bible conceives of the human person as holistic, Christian theology under the influence of Greek philosophy increasingly saw the human in dualistic terms, with the soul being treated with greater importance than the body.[2]

---

[2]   A good example of such dualistic influence in Christian thinking is found in the way Matt. 16:26 is translated in the KJV and the NIV. The word *psyche* which is translated "soul" should properly be translated "life", meaning one's true self. The point that Jesus is making is that one can gain the whole world, and yet lose what is really important in life, which is one's relationship to God and all that salvation includes. But as translated in the KJV and the NIV, the impression is given that what is really important is the salvation of the soul and not the body, which is not at all the meaning intended by Jesus!

At a more fundamental level, the Chinese scholar, Carver Yu (1987), notes that the way in which reality is conceived of in Greek philosophy — as something which is "complete-in-itself, self-subsistent and self-motivating" (67) — means that every reality is complete in itself, and has no need of any interaction or interpenetration with other realities for its existence (78–86). This laid the foundation for the development of individualism in Western thought. A thing, or being, becomes by definition self-subsistent by and of itself, without any need for relation to other things or beings.

This individualistic understanding of being was taken into the foundations of modern Western philosophy through Descartes. In his famous statement "I think, therefore I am", the "I" is a being or substance (using Aristotelian language) who finds meaning and existence in and of itself, without the need for any reference to the external world.[3] As a result, individualism became fully established in Western thought (Yu 1987, 98–105).

This individualism in turn further helped to accentuate the individualisation and spiritualisation of salvation, a tendency that has been endemic in Western theology since Augustine (Bosch 1991, 215–217). By his time, the doctrine of the immortality of the soul was already being taken for granted — one of the clearest indications of the continuing hold of Greek philosophy on Christian theology (Pelikan 1971, 51).[4]

---

[3] In contrast to the Cartesian statement, "I think, therefore I am", the proper Christian alternative would be "I love, therefore I am". Whereas Descartes' statement emphasises individualistic self-consciousness as the foundation for being, the Christian alternative emphasises loving relationship with God, other humans, the created world and oneself as the foundation for being.

For Augustine, salvation is both other-worldly and individualistic, with the primary emphasis given to the redemption of the soul rather than the reconciliation of the world. This, as David Bosch puts it, "could not but spawn a dualistic view of reality, which became second nature in Western Christianity — the tendency to regard salvation as a private matter and to ignore the world" (Bosch 1991, 216). Thus, eventually, Platonic body-soul dichotomy combined together with Cartesian individualism to firmly establish the dualistic view of reality in Western thought, as well as the individualisation and spiritualisation of Christian salvation in Western theology.

The overall result of these developments is that the universe is perceived in dualistic categories at every point: the individual mind and the external world, soul and body, spirit and matter, religious and secular, and so on. The consequence of this on theology and ethics is plain. Instead of thinking holistically, we begin to ask: Is the soul more important or the body? Is salvation spiritual (saving the soul), or physical and sociopolitical (saving the body and society)?

Both liberals and evangelicals (and charismatics) have tended to accept this dualism. Modern liberal Christianity reacted against the spiritualisation of salvation by secularising it. Hence, they deny the importance of

---

4   That the doctrine of the immortality of the soul, which presupposes the body–soul dualism, is alien to biblical thought, which conceives of the person in holistic terms, is clearly brought out by Pelikan's comment: "Indeed, the idea of the immortality of the soul came eventually to be identified with the biblical doctrine of the resurrection of the body, a doctrine one of whose original polemical targets was the immortality of the soul" (Pelikan 1971, 51). The biblical emphasis on the resurrection of the body, in contrast to the Greek idea of the immortality of the soul, is clear from passages like 1 Cor. 1.

evangelism and eternal salvation, and instead emphasise a this–worldly salvation through sociopolitical action alone. On the other hand, many twentieth-century evangelicals have bought into the other side of the dualism. They have accepted the Augustinian tendency to spiritualise and individualise the doctrine of salvation, and have turned it into a purely other-worldly affair with little serious relationship to real life in this world.

Therefore, the tendency for them is to advocate a withdrawal from the "public square" and its concomitant of a "life-boat ethics". The world being sinful is perceived as a sinking ship, hence there is no point in trying to save it. Instead we are to jump into the "life-boat", i.e. the church, and leave the world to sink! (cf. Lovelace 1979, 355–400; esp. 377).

Consequently, many of us (because of our basically evangelical mindset) lack a serious theology of social engagement, which informs and guides us in positive ethical action in a sinful world. To put it in another way, for many Christians our ethics tend to be pietistic and personal, emphasising the "don'ts" more than the "do's". To the extent that ethics is taken seriously — which is not always the case — we tend to emphasise personal holiness in private lives rather than social holiness in public life.

An alien theology

The third inner inadequacy that we face is that Christians in the non-Western world have inherited an alien theology. Even for those of us who may have overcome to some extent the debilitating effect of a dualistic worldview, and have begun to work out a theology that takes social engagement in a sinful world seriously, by and large, most of the answers that we have been given or arrived at have been framed within an "alien" Western context. It is alien in at least two ways.

First, it is alien because the answers are often worked out from the perspective of the West and thus, consciously or subconsciously, prioritise the concerns of the developed world over those of many developing countries in the non-Western world. Take for example, the issue of intellectual property and copyright laws in many areas including books, entertainment, IT hardware and software, drugs, and so forth.

Often it is cheaper to buy a branded mobile device in the West than in many parts of the non-Western world. Even when prices are the same in both developed and developing nations, they are not equitable because of the purchasing power differential between those in rich and those in poorer economies.

Thus, one is forced to ask: In whose interest are intellectual property laws being promulgated and enforced, and to what extent are they just? This is no doubt a complex question because without the proper enforcement of intellectual property rights, R & D in industries will certainly be stifled.

At the same time, unless governments and world trade bodies work harder at making prices more equitable and affordable for poorer nations, the simplistic ethical answer that all intellectual property rights must be respected becomes another form of economic imperialism.[5] One has to ask: In whose interest are copyright laws being promulgated and enforced?

Second, it is alien culturally because the purported answers often fail to take local cultural distinctives into consideration. For example, Christian moral thinking formulated in the West tends to prioritise principles over relationships, on the assumption that decisions are made individually.

But in Asian cultures, relationships are fundamental. A recent article in the *New Straits Times* notes that "In China, *guanxi* (relationship) is everything in business." How then can Christian ethics be worked out in such a situation? Relationships in our cultures are built through gift-giving. But how do we draw the line between a bribe and a gift given in appreciation and/or to cement a relationship?[6]

Another example is that family ties are so close in many Asian societies that charges of nepotism often result (Hamzah-Sendut, *et al.* 1989, 130). Yet, if a Christian fails

---

[5]   Some attempts have been made by world trade bodies to deal with this problem, in particular cases like essential drugs. But much more needs to be done. Otherwise it is simply impossible (not to mention, unjust) to apply intellectual property rules across the board without qualification. This was clearly demonstrated to me just this year when I was teaching a graduate degree course at a fairly well-known seminary in Asia. The students simply took the few books on my prescribed reading list to the photocopying shop next door to print their supply, because they just could not afford to buy the originals. I am not saying this to justify breaking all copyright laws, but rather to highlight the complexity of the ethical issue before us.

[6]   For a helpful introductory discussion on Christian ethics and relationship in the Chinese context, see Tan Che-Bin's *Ethical Particularism as a Chinese Contextual Issue* (1989).

to "take care" of his or her family members, he or she is also damned in the eyes of his or her culture. Obviously, answers developed in the West will need to be rethought in a sensitive manner before they can be applied to another cultural context.[7]

---

[7]   The only book available that explores Christian ethical thinking in a cross-cultural manner is Bernard T. Adeney's *Strange Virtues* (1995). But see Paul G. Hiebert's *Anthropological Insights for Missionaries* (1985) and *Anthropological Reflections on Missiological Issues* (1994) on the crucial importance of taking cultural issues seriously in the proper communication of the gospel and formulation of theology in another culture.

Chapter 2

Developing a Theology of Social Engagement

Any attempt to formulate a theology of social engagement that is both biblical and sensitive to Asian concerns will not be easy. There are no easy, clear-cut answers. Hard work will be required on the part of both the Christian community as a whole, and the individual Christian in his or her respective place of work.

Some Fundamental Principles

First, some fundamental principles need to be clearly set out.

Principle 1: We need to have a clear grasp of the pressures that are confronting us in the world around us, especially in the marketplace, on the one hand, and our human weaknesses and spiritual inadequacies on the other.

Enough has been said on this earlier. The only point that I would like to make here is that, although many of us recognise these issues in theory, we fail to take them seriously in practice. For example, how often do the sermons, Bible studies, etc. in our churches address these issues directly? When was the last time your church did a series of sermons or ran a seminar on holiness or Christian ethics in the modern world?

Again, how many of us, individually, have found the pressures towards compromise too great because our inner spiritual fibres were not strong enough to resist the temptations of ambition and power, money and sex? Hence much more prayer, thought and effort need to be given to these issues in our pastoral practices.

Principle 2: We need to develop a theology of social engagement that firmly rejects an unbiblical dualistic worldview and a withdrawal from the "public square".

We have noted earlier that the dualistic worldview that separates spirit and matter, soul and body, and which leads to a spiritualisation and individualisation of salvation, is unbiblical and a perversion of Christian thinking. God is interested in the salvation of the whole person and the whole universe (Rom. 8:18–23).

The Great Commandment emphasises that the call to love God and "neighbour" are inseparable (Mark 12:29–31; and par.; and also 1 John 4:20f). The Christian is further called to be the "salt of the earth" and the "light of the world" (Matt. 5:13–16 NLT). All these and more point to the need for Christians to have a theology of social engagement which informs Christian ethics and action in a sinful world.

This is particularly needful for those of us who live in an Islamic context. *Islam does not have a dualistic worldview.* It affirms that the *Shariah* is relevant to the whole of life, and not least to the "public square". Indeed, it asserts its superiority over every other worldview or religious faith, and its demand for subservience from all has very severe implications for every non-Muslim living in Islamic lands.

So long as we hold on to a dualistic worldview which leads us to forget about our sociopolitical responsibilities in the world we live in, Christians will always end up with an inadequate apologetic vis-à-vis Islam. Our Muslim friends will always see Christianity as an other-worldly faith that has no relevance to the real world!

It is in part against this background that Professor Lamin Sanneh (1993, 168), an African teaching at Yale, castigates Western Christianity — with its inherently dualistic vision of life — in its present interactions with Islam for losing sight of the Gospel as public truth. This is something that Islam refuses to do, because it is not locked into a dualistic worldview. Christians today urgently need to recover the moral vision of the Bible that affirms its fundamental relevance to both the private and the public spheres of life.

Principle 3: We need to have a clear understanding of Christian moral principles, but appropriately interpreted and applied to our context and culture.

The Bible and Christian theological teachings down the centuries contain a wealth of ethical resources for us to draw on. Many of the fundamental principles of Christian ethics are well known. We need to do two things. First, we need to draw on them. This involves in-depth study of the Bible and Christian ethical thought. But these principles were set in cultures and sociopolitical contexts which are alien to ours. Hence, secondly, we need to interpret these principles in a way that is culturally relevant, and sensitive to the problems faced in our situation.[1]

Take, for example, the problem of bribery and corruption. A bribe has been defined as "an inducement improperly influencing the performance of a public function meant to be gratuitously exercised" (Noonan 1986, 65). But, "What counts as 'an inducement', what counts as 'improperly influencing', what counts as 'a public function', what functions are 'meant to be gratuitously exercised' have changed as culture has changed" (Noonan 1986, 65). In other words, the issues are not as straightforward as we would like them to be.

The Old Testament is very clear on the prohibition of the use of a bribe to pervert justice (Ex. 18:21; 23:8; Deut. 16:19; Amos 5:12; Mic. 7:3; etc.). But it nevertheless recognises that in traditional cultures, gifts are often used to secure favours that may not involve acts of perversion of justice (cf. Gen. 43:11; Mal. 1:8).

Yet the line between a bribe and a gift is not always easy to draw. Serious theological reflection, which also involves a thorough study of cultures and customs, is necessary. This is one task that must be done within the Asian church if we are ever to develop a theology that will inform Christian engagement in the world.

---

[1]   For some helpful literature, see e.g. Christopher Wright's *Living as the People of God* (1983) on Old Testament ethics, Richard Hays' *The Moral Vision of the New Testament* (1996) and Stephen C. Mott's *Biblical Ethics and Social Change* (2011). John Stott's *Issues Facing Christians Today* (2006) is probably the best one-volume Christian study on ethical issues. .

Developing a Theology of Social Engagement: An Incarnational Model

Having noted the above principles, we need to ask what model we should adopt in seeking to put these principles into practice. Robert Webber in his book *The Secular Saint* (1979) helpfully sums up the models that have been developed in Christian thought in history. These are the "Separational Model", the "Identificational Model", and the "Transformational Model" (75–165).

The "Separational Model" draws on biblical emphases like the call for Christians to be "aliens and exiles" in the world (1 Peter 2:11), and to not "love the world" (1 John 2:15). It is characterised in history especially by the pre-Constantinian church, and the Anabaptists. It emphasises the Christian's separation from the world and withdrawal from public life (Webber 1979, 75–104).

The "Identificational Model" draws on Old Testament examples of God's people in public life, like Joseph and Daniel, and on Jesus' incarnation as an expression of his concern to identify with the world in its contradictions. Historically it is represented especially by the Constantinian church and civil religion.

This model sees the Christian as living simultaneously under God's law in two realms, the church and the state (representing the world), since both are ordained by God. But this means that the Christian is often caught in the tension between the two. In the conflicting demands inherent within this model, the danger is for the Christian to slide into accommodation with the world (Webber 1979, 105–134).

The "Transformational Model" draws on images like Christians being "salt" and "light" (Matt. 5:13–16), and is in line with the total thrust of biblical teaching. Historically, it is supremely identified with Augustine and Calvin. This model rejects the idea of withdrawal emphasised by the first model, and that of accommodation which the second model often slips into. It accepts the distinction of the Christian living in two separate realms, the church and the world, but sees the church as being in a position to convert and change the structures of the world into something which is more in tune with God's laws (Webber 1979,135–165).

Webber goes on to note that the basic thrust of each of these three models is rooted in some aspects of biblical teaching, and therefore to emphasise one at the expense of another will lead to an unbalanced approach. Further, he argues that the cultural and sociopolitical contexts may demand an emphasis on one model more than on another (Webber 1979, 184–188). He therefore argues that we should integrate these three models under the "Incarnational Model" (188–201) which is rooted in the way Jesus related to the world. Jesus "*identified* with the world; was *separate* from the ideologies that rule it; and by His death, resurrection, and second coming assured its *transformation*" (188; italics mine).

The basic soundness of Webber's position becomes clear on reflection. For example, with respect to corruption, none of us wishes to identify with the world. But in an imperfect world, none of us can avoid some involvement with it altogether, however indirect, unless one chooses a hermit's existence or a rigid separation model. Just consider: How much of the money you paid for your house was for the purpose of greasing palms? Or, what percentage of the price you paid for a piece of merchandise went to the various corruption practices involved before it reached the market? On the other hand, all of us recognise that separation is a Christian principle. Yet, although we are not of the world, we remain in the world, living with all its contradictions (John 17:14–19; 1 Cor. 5:10).

And as for transformation, we all should do as much as we can to check the spread of corruption. All of us can do, at the very least, a little. For a start, we can stop paying off the police if they were to demand a bribe for traffic infringements; and, in whichever profession we may be in, we can join groups that actively campaign against bribery. But the fact remains that, until Christ returns, corruption will continue to exist in one form or other. This is where we need to learn to pray: "God grant me the serenity to accept the things I cannot change; the courage to change the things I can; and the wisdom to know the difference."[2]

---

[2]   *Serenity Prayer* by Reinhold Niebuhr.

Chapter 3

Applying the "Incarnational Model" In Practice:
The Problem of Bribery and Corruption

We now move on to attempt to sketch out briefly how the incarnational model works in practice. We will use, for illustration, the problem of corruption, which poses the issues involved in the most acute form.[1]

However, before laying out some summary principles, two points need to be clarified. First, the difference between the incarnational model and the separational model needs to be made clear. As argued above, one can only avoid corruption altogether if one applies the separational model rigidly. In practice, very few have succeeded in living in that way. One would have to opt for a hermit's existence or, as in the case of some Anabaptist groups in history, for example the Amish of North America, to opt to live in communities isolated as far as possible from the rest of the world. This

---

[1]   Malaysia has been classed by *The Economist* as a nation in the "middle corruption" category, together with China and Japan. For comparison purposes, Taiwan and Singapore are classed in the "low corruption" category, and Philippines in the "high corruption" category ("Bribonomics").

point needs to be made strongly so that we can be brutally honest about our life in the world. The vast majority of Christians will find themselves "in the world", though not wanting to be "of the world" as well. But once we are "in the world", we cannot pretend that we remain untouched by it.

Once we have chosen the second option, that of being "in the world", i.e. the incarnational model, broadly speaking we then have two options before us. One, which we will call "Alternative 1", is to opt for jobs where it is possible to avoid corruption as much as possible. This would usually mean jobs in government sectors where we can choose not to be touched by corruption. However, even there, things are not always smooth sailing. Temptations abound, and even when you wish to keep yourself above them, you may face intense pressure from colleagues or superiors who may not share your convictions. It could also include certain types of jobs in the marketplace where one is relatively shielded from corrupt practices. This would be true of some professions, for example medicine or law. But even here there are all sorts of potential problems when it comes to getting permits to operate, or getting files moving through the bureaucracies, etc.

The other alternative, "Alternative 2", is the one majority of people in the marketplace have to work in. Here, corruption ranges from the relatively mild to serious, depending on the industry you are in. Examples of these include accountancy, banking, manufacturing, construction, and import-export. Those who opt for jobs in these sectors will find it impossible to avoid some entanglement with corrupt practices, whether directly or indirectly.

The second point that needs clarifying is this. Some people in both "Alternatives 1 & 2" have attempted to "solve" the problem by taking one of the following three ways out. One, "If I am the boss, and paying is the only way to get things moving, I will ask one of my subordinates, a 'friend' or an 'agency' to do it. I don't want to be directly involved." Or, "If the boss asks me to do it, I will do it. But I am not responsible." Or again, "If the boss asks me to do, I still will not do it. But I will ask him to get someone else to do it. I just don't wish to dirty my hands." Careful analysis of each of the above apparent solutions will show that, whether you like it or not, you have to bear part of the responsibility, directly or indirectly. I do not think that we can so easily salve our consciences by putting things in such black-and-white terms.

In other words, one must be clear about one's alternatives. Most of us do not have the luxury of the separational model. We are then left with the incarnational model. But once we adopt this model, there is no way we can avoid all forms of entanglement with corruption, however indirect.

Further, within the incarnational model, we can choose either "Alternative 1 or 2". With "Alternative 1" we will find it relatively easier to keep away from some direct entanglement with corruption at most times, but not necessarily all the time. With "Alternative 2", we will invariably find ourselves being caught up in situations where bribes will be asked for in some form or other.

The proposed guidelines that follow are addressed to those who have adopted the incarnational model, especially those in "Alternative 2".

Guideline 1: The separation principle requires that all forms of active corruption be absolutely prohibited.

It would be helpful to begin by making a distinction between *active corruption*, which involves paying a bribe to get something done illegally and/or immorally, and *passive acceptance* within a corrupt system, which involves paying to get something legitimate moving faster. All Christians would affirm that the former must be strictly prohibited. This would include, for example, the following:

i. Receiving bribes in any form for oneself to do something unjust or illegal for someone else.
ii. Giving bribes in any form to secure something unjustly or illegally for oneself.
iii. Outright lies and dishonesty.
iv. Sexual immorality.
v. Outright exploitation of workers.
vi. Defective products.

Guideline 2: The separation principle means that we should avoid as much as possible any form of passive acceptance of corruption.

If the first kind of corrupt practice is strictly prohibited, I would like to argue that the second should be avoided as much as possible, although total avoidance will be impossible. I am aware that I am advocating a position here that does not view everything in black-and-white terms. For the lack of a better term, I have used the term *passive acceptance* to describe this position. Many will baulk at any suggestion of such a thought, because we are used to seeing things in black and white and this smacks of compromise. Perhaps the following comments will help.

i. First, I have already argued that once we adopt the incarnational model, we cannot avoid some forms of *passive acceptance* of corruption in life. To think otherwise is to be untruthful to the facts of life.

ii. My second comment is that a careful reading of the Bible shows that whilst God's moral demands are absolute, a certain degree of accommodation to human weaknesses is found in the way they are applied in real-life situations. For example, the Bible is consistent throughout that monogamy is God's ethical ideal for humanity. Yet, there is not a single direct condemnation of polygamy in the Old Testament. But, in time, the Jews came to see clearly the full implications of Old Testament teaching, and monogamy was the norm by Jesus' time. God appears to be prepared to wait hundreds of years to allow His Word to have its leavening effect on a culture and a people.

Or, consider the problem of slavery. Nowhere do we find any direct criticisms on the institution of slavery, not even in the New Testament. But there are clearly indirect critiques in Galatians 3:28 and Philemon. Yet, after some two thousand years, there is now unanimous agreement amongst Christians that slavery is immoral.

Perhaps the most relevant example to our subject is Jesus' attitude towards the Roman taxation system. The latter was a widely known form of corruption. The collection of taxes was farmed out by the Romans to tax collectors, who often made loads of money on the side (cf. Zacchaeus in Luke 19:1–10). Yet, having challenged the corruption of the system through his conversion of Zacchaeus, Jesus nevertheless stated that taxes (with all the extras going towards corruption) must still be paid — "give to Caesar what belongs to Caesar" (Luke 20:25 NLT).

In each of the above examples, we find a form of *passive acceptance* of the corruption of life in the world. Radical as the Christian message is, there is also a recognition in the Bible that not everything can be changed overnight. There appears to be situations in which God seems prepared to give a society time (sometimes thousands of years) to work at changes gradually. Recognition of the above means that, in dealing with the second form of corruption in the marketplace (that of *passive acceptance*), Christians will need a similar wisdom.

iii. The third comment is that wisdom is specially needed because, as we have already noted, the line between a gift and a bribe is often not clear in non-Western cultures. The law may say that the latter is illegal, but social customs may require the giving of the former. Many Christians do not realise that the tension surrounding this complex issue was also felt in the Old Testament. Thus, for example, in six references to bribery in Proverbs, three condemn it (15:27; 17:23; 22:16), but three others extol it in positive terms (17:8; 18:16; 21:14)! More importantly, every condemnation of bribery in the Bible is directed either at those who practise it to pervert justice, or those who use their positions of power to oppress others, especially the poor. We do **not** find a single condemnation of those who have to pay because they are in a position of weakness and are forced to do so. As Bernard T. Adeney (1995, 152) writes,

> Such equivocation in the Old Testament seems to reflect a recognition of the power differential between a poor person who gives a gift in order to stave off injustice and the rich who uses his power to exploit the poor. The powerful and the powerless are not judged by the same abstract absolute, but by the relationships and intentions of their situation.

In light of the above three comments, the way forward appears to be that, as far as possible, we should avoid any direct involvement, even with respect to the *passive acceptance* of corruption. This would mean that if we are in the position of the boss, we should always view that as the very last resort. It should never be used as a shortcut to avoid the hard work to find every legitimate means of solving the problem. Or, if we are under orders, we may need to say to the boss, at the risk of incurring his wrath or even losing our jobs, "Please get someone else to do it."

However, in doing so we must always remember two things. First, when taking this position, we must avoid any sense of personal moral superiority on our part, which allows us to be judgemental towards those who are directly involved. For whether we are directly or indirectly involved, we share in the sinfulness of that action — in so far as it is less than God's ideal. Secondly, by saying that we would rather not do it, we are making a point, that we do not believe that this is ultimately the basis upon which our society should be built. There is something improper about such actions. And ideally this should not have to be. Ultimately, it is still the Christian's goal to wipe it out for the good of all. This leads to the third guideline.

Guideline 3: The incarnational model would require that we practise identification only to the extent that it allows us to work for transformation.

Some systems are so inherently corrupt that it would seem impossible to effect any transformation from within. The Gestapo of Nazi Germany or the ex-Soviet KGB would be good examples from recent history. In the early church, by the end of the second century, the church generally took the line that Christians should not be in the civil service, the military or in the Roman entertainment industry (charioteers, gladiators, etc.).

This was because the occupations involved idolatry and emperor worship, extreme cruelties, and often killing which is seen as murder (Webber 1979, 80–83). In present-day Asia, the same would apply to businesses and corporations that are founded on an inherently corrupt basis. The only Christian course of action would be to get out in such cases.

In other situations that are more "grey", one would have to weigh the various options carefully. Would staying allow me to effect some socioeconomic or even moral transformation that is for the common good of all? For example, would accepting a low level of *passive corruption* strengthen my ability or my company's ability to provide employment for some needy persons (who would otherwise be unemployed) or better quality of service for the general public?

To many Christians this raises an ugly question. Are we compromising our ethical principles? My response is a firm "No"! For apart from all the other arguments I have already put forth earlier, I would like to draw attention to another principle in Scripture. Consider the episode described in Jeremiah 38:14–28. Jeremiah lies (vv. 24, 27) to a group of evil men to protect the king's position and his own life. This appears to be morally justified. It is comparable to telling an enraged man with a gun looking for a particular person to kill that the person is somewhere else, even when you know where that person actually is. Your responsibility to save life in that situation takes precedence over your responsibility to tell the truth.

One evangelical ethicist, Norman L. Geisler, speaks of the need for a "graded absolutism" in our ethical thinking (1989, 113–132). God's various moral commands are absolute, but they are not all at the same level of importance. To tell a lie in order to save a life in certain (and not just any) circumstances is to recognise that life-saving is more important than truth-telling in God's hierarchy of values.

This does not mean that lying is right in and of itself. Neither does it mean that we are compromising God's law that tells us, "You shall not bear false witness". But in exceptional circumstances, not telling the truth is the lesser of two evils! A "tragic choice" is involved. The right answer in such a situation can only be found through carefully weighing the context and the consequences of each course of action, together with much prayer and wisdom.[2]

In seeking a solution to the problem of corruption, we need to recognise that the same principle of a "graded absolutism" is applicable here. Does our Christian responsibility to the wider public take precedence over the acceptance of a relatively low level of *passive acceptance* of corruption in the system? Does it allow me to work in the longer term to effect some genuine transformation in society, along the lines of the values of the Kingdom of God? Or have I to opt out of the marketplace altogether because it has become so inherently corrupt that the only legitimate form of Christian witness is the "separational model"? These are hard questions. But they need to be faced, not by Christian individuals as individuals, but as members of a pastorally supportive and prayerful community.

This last point is often forgotten by us when struggling with this issue. Trying to resolve such issues alone by oneself opens one up to all sorts of folly and pitfalls. Moreover within any one church, there probably are at least several individuals facing similar challenges in their workplaces. This is where Christians, as members of the Kingdom community and Body of Christ, must help each other to work through such issues together. Apart from the theological point that this is how Christians should live, there are

---

[2]   Bernard T. Adeney (1995,153–156) is dissatisfied with Geisler's idea of "graded absolutism" for various reasons. He argues for an approach which sees God's laws as "*prima facie*" rules which "ought to be absolutes in all cultures and all times" (153). They may "only be broken to avert some greater evil. Unlike situation ethics, *prima facie* rules and principles are not nullified by moral calculation. They remain strong guides for behavior which must be reckoned with even when we tragically break them" (154).

at least three distinct advantages: collective wisdom in approaching the problems, honest discussions that protect us from slipping into easy compromises and foolish rationalisations, and communal and pastoral support for every individual who has to make the tough decisions.

Guideline 4: It may be that different Christians, after genuinely seeking God's mind, will find themselves emphasising different aspects of the "incarnational model" and end up taking different approaches. In such a situation, we must avoid being judgemental towards one another. God may call us to different callings.

God's gifts to us are different and so is His calling. Some may find that the marketplace is altogether too distasteful and opt for a model of total separation. For example, the Anabaptists and their spiritual descendants today, the Mennonites, have always tended towards this position. It may be that God is calling forth some in Asia to do the same, setting up Christian counter-communities as a means of showing the world something more of the values of the Kingdom of God. I am not aware of any such communities within the Protestant churches in Malaysia today. But the Catholic monastic orders have always tended in that direction. And when we think of Mother Theresa's ministry, we may well need to ask why we are so slow in developing Christian counter-cultural communities within our churches today. And is our slowness an indication of our unwillingness to follow the call of the Master to a radical obedience?

On the other hand, Christ calls others to be fully immersed in our fallen world, caught up constantly in all its contradictions. But even so, we may be called to different paths of Christian obedience. For example, I am aware that some Christians have been able to tell marvellous stories of how they have been able to avoid corruption in situations where bribery is unavoidable. This is certainly highly laudable and must be encouraged at every point. However, certain things must be borne in mind before we make this into an absolute standard by which we judge everyone else.

First, those in this category are usually Christians who are more mature in their faith and have grown deep in their prayer life. They need to remember that many other church members are still struggling to arrive at their level of spiritual maturity. They will need time to grow in faith and trust. We must be careful not to lay an impossible load upon their fragile consciences before they are ready. That would be pastorally irresponsible.

Secondly, such people are often in the upper echelons of the business world. They have friends in high places with whom they fraternise regularly at business or government functions, or in golf clubs. Through prayer and such avenues of influence, they find that they can get many things done without paying (anything?). But again we need to remember that the majority of the population does not have such privileges. This is particularly true of blue-collar workers, like taxi-drivers, and small businessmen, like hawkers. These people have a different power relationship to those in positions of authority. When they are victimised by having to pay to get their licences renewed for example, they cannot call on their friends in high places to *selesai* ("settle" in Bahasa Malaysia) the matter for them. And if they do not pay, their licence renewals are held up for long stretches. How then do they feed their families?

Each Christian, with the support of his or her church, must decide what God is calling him or her to. Whatever approaches to the problem that God calls us to, when conscientiously followed, can be just as difficult and costly, and may end up just as powerful in its witness.

Guideline 5: In all these we must never lose sight of the transformation principle, built on the Christian's calling to be "salt" and "light".

It is important to emphasise that the position advocated here is not one of unprincipled compromise. Rather, it is a position firmly rooted in principled arguments. Further, it is also a position that tries to look honestly at the facts of the case and does not try to pretend that we can live in a sterilised world, untouched totally by its moral contradictions. It does not provide easy, straightforward answers in many cases, but neither is it meant to be taken as a licence for unbridled corruption in the corporate world. In all these, the goal of moral and sociopolitical transformation must always be kept in sight.

But the question must be asked: Is transformation possible? Can a situation of endemic corruption be turned round? What hope is there long term? A lesson from history is helpful. In a book, *Corruption in Developing Countries*, first published in the 1963, the authors, Ronald Wraith and Edgar Simpkins, pointed out that Britain at the beginning of the nineteenth century was as corrupt as many non-Western countries today. Yet by about 1880, it came to attain "a standard of public integrity which is perhaps without precedent" (9). This came as a result of the emergence of what has been called "Victorian morality", which persisted till the immediate post-World War II years.[3]

The British historian, Harold Perkin, described this moral change in British society rather more humorously (and also more cynically): "Between 1780 and 1850 the English ceased to be one of the most aggressive, brutal, rowdy, outspoken, riotous, cruel and bloodthirsty nations in the world and became one of the most inhibited, polite, orderly, tender-minded, prudish and hypocritical" (Perkin 2002, 280). What brought these changes about?

Wraith and Simpkins recognised that various factors contributed to the widespread eradication of corruption, including political, socioeconomic, educational, and other changes and advances. Nevertheless they also drew attention to the underlying religious influences that led to the moral changes and deep-seated integrity in the personal and public life of many individuals. They argued that, "It seems that whatever may have been the political and economic reasons for the decline of corruption, the puritanical thread in the fabric of Victorian England was important" (62).

This puritanical thread goes back to the seventeenth century Puritans, who had sought in their time to revive

---

[3]   An interesting and commonly reported example of this phenomenon was when the first Prime Minister of Singapore, the late Lee Kuan Yew, arrived in London in the late 1940s. He was surprised to find newspapers piled up on the streets with no one in attendance. Buyers just took the papers and left the money in a coin box nearby. Try doing that in Malaysia or Singapore, or for that matter, in London today!

English Christianity. But the more important and immediate influence in this thread was the eighteenth century Evangelical Revival under John Wesley and his fellow Methodists.

As Wraith and Simpkins sum up, "The Methodist movement and its aftermath coincided with the industrial revolution and was more largely responsible than any other influence for the integrity and thrift of a large section of the working class" (181). They further argue that the influence of the Methodists and their fellow nonconformists[4] was augmented in the nineteenth century by groups within the Anglican Church which impacted much more the upper classes (180).

Also about this time, the radical philosophers or Utilitarians, particularly Jeremy Bentham and J. S. Mill, came on the scene. They began to apply systematically in public life, their simple utilitarian formula: "the greatest happiness of the greatest number" (182), as the measure for justice and social reform within the nation.

Wraith and Simpkins sum up their discussion of the above influences by arguing that all these flowed as different tributaries into one powerful stream and, working in tandem, eventually pushed much of the corruption out of public life. Without these forces working in Britain in the nineteenth century, "it is questionable whether corruption would have been virtually destroyed by the century's end." They further suggest that corruption in many developing

---

[4] The term "nonconformist" in English history applies to those Protestants who are not Anglicans but belong to the so-called sectarian groups like Congregationists, Baptists, Quakers and later the Methodists.

countries can be eradicated only if "influences as profound as these have worked themselves into the national consciousness" (182).

The finer points of Wraith and Simpkins' thesis can no doubt be debated endlessly. For more details on this, the reader will have to refer elsewhere.[5] But their arguments, taken together with those of other scholars, make it clear that at least three major overlapping influences worked together to bring about the changes.

First, there was the impact of Wesley and the eighteenth century Methodist revival which was sustained well into the nineteenth century. One of Wesley's two life-long goals was to "spread scriptural holiness over the land." On this, he was certainly successful among the working class and the expanding middle class of the nineteenth century.

Second, the Utilitarians also contributed significantly to social reform through their demand for accountability and professionalism in public life and service. As Perkin put it, "Bentham stood above all for efficient, responsible government, what J. S. Mill called 'the combination of complete popular control over public affairs, with the greatest attainable perfection of skilled agency'" (2002, 269).

The third was the impact of the Anglican Evangelicals, William Wilberforce and his colleagues in the Clapham Sect, who significantly influenced the upper classes in moral reformation, and the Parliament and nation in

---

[5]   Other than Wraith and Simpkins (1963), see also Perkin (2002), especially pp. 218–339.

social and legal reform.[6] Indeed, the Clapham Sect and the Utilitarians often worked together, both in and out of Parliament, in their campaigns against corruption and other sociopolitical evils of the time.

Living in Malaysia, or in other countries which are similarly multi-religious and multi-ethnic, how we appropriate and apply the lessons from the British story will be have to be carefully thought through. But two clear lessons can immediately be drawn.

The first is that, like the Utilitarians in British history, there are many in our societies from outside the church who are also concerned about issues of corruption. We need to genuinely appreciate their concerns and contributions. More than that, like Wilberforce and his colleagues, we need to learn to work in cooperation with such people, who may be of different faiths and creeds, for the common good of all in our land.

The second lesson is to remember that Christians can make a difference. As noted above, both the seventeenth and eighteenth century revivalist streams of English Christianity, together with the Anglican Evangelicals in the nineteenth century came together in history to exert a powerful influence for moral reform in the battle against corruption. Wesley was very conscious in his mission about the need to spread "scriptural holiness" over the land, and demanded the highest standards of holy living among the early Methodists. In Wilberforce case, soon after his con-

---

[6]   On the work and impact of William Wilberforce and the Clapham Sect, see Bradley (1976), Pollock (1977) and Tomkins (2010).

version to Christianity, he came to the clear conviction that "God Almighty has set before me two great objects, the suppression of the Slave Trade and the Reformation of Manners (i.e. moral values)". On both counts, history shows that he succeeded brilliantly. The challenge to us is to produce a generation of men and women who are similarly clear about God's calling to do the same in the church and in public life today.

Some readers may respond by saying that it is too much today to have to wait for the streams of Christian revival and moral renewal to flow for two to three centuries, as they did in Britain, before we can hope to see change in our societies. Surely we have to act NOW!

I cannot agree more. And that is exactly the point. Wilberforce came to the clear conviction of God's call to battle slavery and to work at national moral reform in 1787. He stuck to this calling for the next forty-five years, dying within days of Parliament's passing the slavery abolition bill in 1832. It was the work of a lifetime — his task was done!

Wesley on the other hand was not the immediate player in the twin drama of national moral reform and the battle against slavery. But the evidence is there that his ministry paved the way for Wilberforce and the Clapham Sect — especially by demanding the highest standards of holiness in lives of Christians. Each accomplished what God gave them to do in one lifetime. This can also be true of us — we do not have to wait for God to work over two to three centuries!

Corruption will continue to be rife unless there is a fundamental change in private lives of individuals and the public conscience of our nation. So we must pray and work for revival so that individual lives will come to know true repentance and moral transformation. But that alone will not be enough if we continue to hold on to a dualistic theology which prevents us from relating the values of the Kingdom of God to the burning ethical and sociopolitical issues of our day. Sociopolitical problems cannot merely be spiritualised and then simply exorcised away!

Hence, we will also need to pray that God will raise up Christians, like Wesley and Wilberforce, who will seize the initiative in the battle against sin and corruption, and work to bring about holiness in the church and moral reformation in our land.

Conclusion

G od calls His people, not just to save individual souls, but also to bring Kingdom values to bear on the sociopolitical issues of the day. Such a task will require Christians who are willing to respond to Christ's call to live lives of radical obedience. We need to ask God for grace to enable us to stand firm against the temptations of money, sex and power.

We need further to ask Him for wisdom to develop a holistic worldview and a theology of social engagement. And we need to seek from Him spiritual power and moral authority. Without these we will wilt and fall in the battle against the powers of darkness, which continue to keep so many societies in our world in the bondage of corruption. But if through God's empowering we can bring holiness to the church and moral reformation to the country, then the Malaysian church will truly be "salt" and "light" in this land, helping to transform it into a godly, righteous, just and prosperous nations.

One last thought: Does this mean that a whole society has to become Christian before corruption can be got rid of? Not at all! It is worth pointing out that even at its highest point of influence in the nineteenth century, the evangelical revival of the eighteenth century reached only about six to seven per cent of England's total population. Yet its impact was nationwide.

Robert Bellah, a sociologist who used to teach at the University of California, Berkeley, has suggested that we often underestimate the influence of a small committed minority in society. He argues that, "The quality of a culture may be changed when two percent of its people have a new vision" (quoted in Stott 1984, 76). Surely this is a challenge worth taking up!

SECTION 2 *THEOLOGICAL RESPONSES*

Chapter 4

Response *by* Albert M. Erisman

Seattle Pacific University
Seattle, Washington, USA

How should Christians look at doing business in parts of the world where the incidence of bribery and corruption is high? Two approaches are common from a Western perspective. The first is to avoid doing business in these places. The second is to treat business as a "Monday" institution, and recognise these issues as just a part of doing business in that part of the world. Christianity is a "Sunday" thing and has little to do with business.

The first approach is wrong on many counts. For those who live in these regions, this may be the only way to make a living. Of course, there are professions that would seem to be out of bounds for Christians, but as we shall see, simply withdrawing from the world is neither practical nor biblical. Further, ethics is about doing good — business ethics is about doing good in business. I often remind my students that avoiding doing bad is very different from doing good. Ethics is more than just avoiding bad things. If we avoid doing business in difficult areas, we may be condemning these people to poverty and want. Jesus came to bring hope to the poor, and we should be agents of that hope. We see that Jesus came into the world at a time and place of great corruption, including in the tax system. He brought Matthew out of the system, transformed Zacchaeus in the system, and continued to pay His taxes in spite of the system. We are called to bring hope and healing to a world that is broken, not to duck the difficult challenges.[1]

But the second approach is wrong as well. We are whole people who cannot divide our world into compartments. Work is a part of the calling of God, and our daily work is an integral part of who we are as humans. One of the big outcomes of sin as seen in Genesis 3 is the disintegration of our lives, breaking it into compartments with the divide between the sacred and the secular — a dualistic worldview. As agents of the Kingdom of God, we are called to bring hope to our world. Bribery and corruption are a result of sin, and dealing with these is a part of what we are called to do in our world.

Hwa's Key Points

Hwa Yung has been careful to avoid the two extremes cited above in his excellent paper. He has taken on the significant challenge of dealing with the reality of ethics (in particular bribery and corruption), rather than avoiding the cultural interaction or living dualistically. He has called us to an incarnational life. As such, this paper is a significant contribution to biblical thinking, and can be the basis for the transformation of many communities,

---

[1]   "Case Studies in Business Ethics" by Albert M. Erisman, seminar at Urbana 2006, the InterVarsity Christian Fellowship Missions Conference, St. Louis, MO., December 30, 2006.

bringing the principles of the Kingdom of God to our world. It will be of great help to our brothers and sisters in regions where there is rampant corruption. They need some clear guidance, and this paper lays an important part of the foundation for this guidance. But the value of it is not limited to those in the so-called "corrupt" regions. It is equally important to those in the West for two quite different reasons. First, there is a tendency for us in the West to point the finger without understanding the problem. The careful analysis is helpful, enabling us to be more empathetic to this real-world challenge.

Secondly, as we read this paper we may become much more aware of the corruption in our own systems. Perhaps the bribery and corruption are not as open, but they are as real. Ultimately, we must see ourselves in this mirror, not simply see a solution to a distant problem. This point is particularly clear in the section of the document talking about the line between a gift and a bribe.

I spent 32 years at a large multinational corporation, and it was clear that we would be fired if we took a bribe. But it was not unusual to see executives being taken to dinners by vendors. Even more subtle is the case of a purchasing agent who must choose between two vendors and will need to visit the winning vendor frequently once the choice is made. How is that purchasing agent influenced in his decision by the relative attractiveness of the cities where these vendors are located? More blatantly in the West, the Enron crisis has now been followed by the financial crisis. Both are a clear witness to the challenge of ethics in business in the West.

In his paper, Hwa is very careful to observe that we cannot provide simple answers to complex problems. In particular, he says:

> "We find a form of passive acceptance of the corruption of life in the world. Radical as the Christian message is, there is also a recognition in the Bible that not everything can be changed overnight."

This does not mean either accommodation or acceptance of bribery and corruption. Hwa challenges us to deal openly with the clear tension of these issues.

This observation reminds us of a fundamental concept in ethics: "It is not just about me, and it is not just about right now." In our technologically infused world, we have developed a "now" mentality. It would appear that what Jesus did in his dealings with the tax system laid the groundwork for future, more fair, and transparent systems while understanding that change is a process. It is helpful in this analysis that Hwa takes the long-term view and does not shy away from the apparent tensions in dealing biblically in this environment.

Other Considerations

I would encourage readers of this paper to start with what Hwa has provided but move beyond it in many ways. Here are eight:

1. In the beginning, he focuses on the three factors that act as external pressures against us in the challenge of ethical dealings: money, sex, and power. While these

forces are indeed powerful, I believe Speed (in part due to technology enabling our world to move much faster), Consumerism (there is never enough) and Prestige (the desire not just for power but to do a good job) are three other strong forces. A broader agenda would both add to the analysis and strengthen his approach.

2. The focus on bribery and corruption is important given the context of the paper. But ethics is a much broader topic, extending to fair wages, treatment of the environment, caring for employees, avoiding the exploitation of workers (including women and children), etc. It would be helpful to broaden the discussion to include these topics also.

3. One topic Hwa raises briefly is intellectual property. Unfortunately, his brief comment is not very helpful in exploring the applicability and abuse of IP. In particular, within a capitalistic system there is a need for financial incentives related to research and development. What are the unintended consequences of eliminating these incentives? Would new discoveries continue or dry up? In the information technology field, for example, we see "open source" software operating alongside proprietary software, where users get a choice. That many continue to use proprietary software testifies to the importance of the research and development. This is a topic worthy of much more discussion than is given. And it has a very important side impact. With today's laws in place, and with the present practice where parts of the world readily copy and distribute IP, does this have a corrosive effect on character as people willingly break the law?

4. While it is true that much material on ethics has been developed in the West, and may not be specific about issues in the developing world, I would argue that at the right level, it is more relevant than Hwa identifies. At the level of principle, there is much we can share. As we get more specific, this is where we must be more focused on the context.

   Hwa does a nice job of identifying some of the cultural characteristics that make specific ethical decision-making different between the West and the developing world. A broader study of this would be helpful, at least through references. There are two references I have found helpful in this area. A secular view of the subject is developed in *The Asian Crisis*.[2] A biblical view is developed in a study by the Bakke Graduate University.[3]

5. Making ethical decisions is best done with counsel and not by ourselves. Our ability to rationalise a poor decision is too great. This is why a fundamental tenet of ethics involves engaging others. The more senior the leaders, the more isolated they tend to become. For the Christian leader, it is imperative that he or she is surrounded by a group who can act as a sounding board for ethical decisions. So I would emphasise the communal aspect of ethical decision-making more than Hwa did. He laid the groundwork for this in his recognition of the more individualistic West, but needs

---

[2]   Frank Jurgen Richter and Pamela C.M. Mar. *Asia's New Crisis: Renewal Through Total Ethical Management*. Singapore: John Wiley and Sons (Asia), 2004.

[3]   "A Contextualized Theology of Work for Asia: an expanded summary deriving from discussions during the Asian consultation on Marketplace Theology", Manila, sponsored by the Bakke Graduate University, notes by Paul Stevens, November 28–30, 2007.

to carry this through to the decision-making process.

6. It is often helpful to have a specific process for making an ethical decision. Many of these are available, but one we use at Seattle Pacific University is:

   a. *What are the ethical issues in the current situation?*
   b. *What is the appropriate law?*
   c. *What are the relevant values and principles that can be brought to bear on the situation?*
   d. *What are the potential consequences of the decisions that might be made?*
   e. *Who can provide counsel to clarify the issues and possible decisions?*
   f. *Take action.*

7. Hwa suggests that the topic of ethics is important if we are to engage the world, since the alternative of withdrawing is not acceptable. I would add a question here: where would we withdraw to?

   It is my experience that so-called safer, Christian settings can also be challenging environments in which to practise the ethical principles in our work. The problems may be more subtle, but they are very real. The danger often is that we have our guard down because we believe we are in a "safe haven" and don't even recognise the ethical challenges we should be resolving.

8. Finally, I believe Hwa did an excellent job of identifying the importance of our daily work as a part of who we are before God. He rightly recognised that we hear far too few sermons that would be specifically helpful to

a leader in an ethical situation. However, I believe he stopped short of discussing what the Scripture has to say about our work — I believe that Hwa builds his case for time in this world, but not for eternity. If we hold to the idea that our work is good for this world, but only our relationships survive to eternity, then this will impose a hierarchy on the relative importance of the work we do and the relationships we hold. Though our work becomes instrumental to other priorities, it necessarily slips back to being of secondary importance because it is for time, whereas "spiritual matters" are for eternity.

Two authors who challenge this thesis are Darrel Cosden (*The Heavenly Good of Earthly Work*)[4] and N. T. Wright (*Surprised by Hope*).[5] These authors argue that our work is not only temporally important but eternally important. If this is so, it changes our perspective on why decisions of acting ethically in society are so important.

Are they done so that we can be a good witness to those around us and influence them for the Kingdom? Yes, of course. But are they also done because the things we do every day count, in and of themselves, for eternity? Cosden and Wright would argue that it is so. And if it is, then how we conduct ourselves in our daily lives has a much more urgent character. Our faith affects our work not just "so that"; rather, our daily work lasts for eternity.

---

[4]   Darrell Cosden. *The Heavenly Good of Earthly Work*. Peabody, MA: Hendrickson Publishers, 2006.

[5]   N. T. Wright. *Surprised by Hope: Rethinking Heaven, the Resurrection, and the Mission of the Church*. New York, NY: HarperCollins, 2008.

Conclusion

In spite of these suggestions, however, I believe that Hwa's contribution is excellent. He forces us all to step beyond our dualism, to move past giving simple answers to complex questions, and to be humble in accepting that a brother or sister in another part of the world might make a decision that is different from the one we make in another context. I trust this book will be an inspiration, and a reason for hope, for all of those called by God to work in a setting where the path forward is neither easy nor clear. I would encourage readers to get together and discuss this book, talking openly about the personal application of it to the specific contexts they face. I believe this would be a great step in bringing the principles of the Kingdom of God to our world, so that "they may see our good deeds and glorify our Father who is in Heaven".

Chapter 5

Response *by*
L. T. Jeyachandran

Former Executive Director
Ravi Zacharias International Ministries (Asia-Pacific)

The paper written by Bishop Hwa Yung, although from a Malaysian perspective, is applicable to Christians everywhere. Having worked for almost 29 years with the Indian government and for another 15 years with a Christian organisation, I feel that the question of integrity among Christians — in the marketplace or in the Church — is an issue of great concern. There is the distinct possibility that integrity has largely been replaced by Christian activism and our influence in the world as salt and light has become minimal.

Bishop Hwa begins the first part of his paper with a reference to three external pressures Christians face: covetousness (lust of the eyes), temptations of the flesh (lust of the flesh) and the lust for power and control (boasting of what a person has and does). These compare admirably with the three avenues of temptation outlined by John (1 John 2:16) and the three temptations of Eve (Gen. 3:6) and the Lord Jesus (Matt. 4:1–10; Luke 4:1–12). I found this section very helpful because, even after walking with the Lord for many years, it is frightening to realise how the values of the fallen world system can find a lodging place in one's subconscious in the most horrific and insidious manner! It is also significant that all the temptations we face come only from these three quarters and from nowhere else!

The next part of the paper deals with three inner inadequacies:

1. As stated in the paragraph above, I find this emphasis on the "inner corruption of the soul" very timely. I have observed in Christian circles today that there is, sadly, greater concern with unhealed sicknesses than with unconquered sins. We also do not have people with whom we can share our inmost struggles as we long for victory in our pilgrim journey. Instead, what we have are prayer meetings that offer instant answers!

2. I cannot agree more with the author in his depiction of our world-denying theology as that of a "life-boat". It almost sounds as if we are preparing people to die (in order to go to "heaven") but not to live in this world which happens to have been created by God. I have come to the conclusion that the theology of the average Christian begins with Genesis 3 and ends with Revelation 20 — it begins with the Fall and ends with the Judgement. Because we omit four important chapters (Gen. 1 & 2; Rev. 21 & 22) in the development of our theology, our view of creation — the present one created by God, and the renewal of this one at the climax of human history — is extremely weak, even if our understanding of redemption is quite orthodox.

   I am afraid that we are not connecting with the outside world because our message of redemption hangs limp, since it does not latch on to the real, material world. The point of Bishop Hwa's paper is that the right theology should be evidenced by the right praxis and that is the royal route to communicating the Christian faith to the outside world. During my years in the Indian government service, four Old Testament characters were my role models — Joseph, Daniel, Esther and Nehemiah. They were in the marketplace under non-Jewish governments, and worked with integrity even in their country of exile.

3. I agree with Bishop Hwa's third point in this context — an alien theology — for somewhat different reasons. Western views and values arise out of an individualist view of life, whereas our Eastern view has a central place for the communal nature of reality. Thanks to globalisation, our part of the world has also become increasingly individual-oriented but its way of looking at moral issues from a communal angle has not been totally eclipsed.

My submission at this point is that the understanding of God as Trinity combines the individual with the communal — how this view of God, and therefore of reality, should reflect on ethics is a matter for Christians to painstakingly work out and exhibit in our lives.

The second part of Bishop Hwa's paper begins with his statement of three fundamental principles:

1. As I have already mentioned above, our struggle against and victory over sin is not an attractive topic in these times; in emphasising free grace, some circles

make it cheap. All of us to whom God has delegated the responsibility of leadership of some sort will have to take note of this aspect of the biblical message.

2. I was pleasantly surprised by Bishop Hwa's use of the phrase "Gospel and public truth" which was popularised by my former Bishop in the Church of South India, Lesslie Newbigin. I am not quite in agreement with Bishop Hwa's analysis of Islam — in my understanding, Islam does not have a spiritual dimension at all and therefore it is not surprising that it is not dualistic. For us, the problem of dualism is a real one because, as humans, we are a combination of **matter** and **spirit** and we have to live in the tension between the **now** and **not yet** — creatures of **time** longing for **eternity**! Our challenge is therefore all the greater because we need to hold both realities — spirit and matter, time and eternity — in a healthy Biblical tension.

3. I totally agree with Bishop Hwa's emphatic point that Christian moral principles of Scripture "should be appropriately interpreted and applied to our context and culture". In my country, India, and as I can understand from this paper, in Malaysia as well, payment is often demanded even for granting what is one's legitimate right and when all legal or bureaucratic requirements have been met. I would prefer to term this as "extortion" rather than a "bribe" which, in John T. Noonan Jr.'s definition, is an "inducement improperly influencing the performance of a public function meant to be gratuitously exercised".[1] To be sure, the line that divides the two is a thin one and the former can

---

[1]   Noonan, John T., Jr. "Bribery". In *A New Dictionary of Christian Ethics*, eds. John Macquarrie and James Childress. Philadelphia, PA: Westminster Press, 1986, 65f.

sometimes function as the thin end of the wedge of the latter; but having said that, one should still differentiate between the two. The refusal to make the distinction can, on the one hand, result in a hypocritical, legalistic and smug satisfaction that we have obeyed (more than) the letter of the law. On the other hand, it can result in a burdened conscience in the Christian who is struggling to live an upright life and who is forced to pay an extortion to preserve his and his employees' livelihoods.

The incarnational model is the right way to go because our Lord and Master went before us in the same way. We have no record of the pressures under which he found Himself in his business as carpenter. The five guidelines given in the paper and the accompanying examples are very illustrative. They also demonstrate the impossibility of not being touched by the world in some way if we choose to remain in it.

The reference to paying taxes to Caesar is eloquent — where acceptance of a passive form of corruption is shown as inescapable in a fallen world. Similarly, the quote from Bernard Adeney on the references to bribery in the book of Proverbs, and the quote from Norman Geisler on "graded absolutism" should be necessary ingredients in all our teaching and practice of ethics.

The freedom for the Christian to choose her/his level of involvement in society is admirably treated. The conclusion that true moral transformation of society cannot be effected unless there is a spiritual revival is well made. Bishop Hwa has truly performed the duty of the watchman by sounding the right note in the right trumpet at the right time!

Chapter 6

Response *by* David W. Gill

Founder and Principal
EthixBiz Consulting

Let me begin by applauding Hwa Yung's great effort and accomplishment in this paper. It is certainly a worthy contribution to a very important challenge. It strikes me as both faithful to Scripture and practical/insightful for working Christians in the marketplace.

Obviously, no two authors would (or could) approach a topic in exactly the same way. I will give you my perspective on the topics raised but it should be understood that my remarks are simply the observations of a friend and colleague from a distance. Hwa Yung is much closer to the specific problems and contexts he addresses and I yield to his expertise.

External Pressures & Internal Inadequacies

The External Pressures: Money, Sex, and Power

I agree that money, sex, and power are three particularly strong temptations and that they are inadequately addressed by today's preaching and teaching. In my own view (discussed in my book, *Becoming Good: Building Moral*

Character), however, a deeper insight is provided by the three temptations of Christ, which are a comprehensive rubric for all the temptations and tests of life: stones into bread (relating to the self & its appetites); the kingdoms of the world and their glory (relating to others, our neighbours); and leaping off the temple (relating to God). Jesus is our model. He was tested on all points like we are. Money, sex and power are "species" of these temptations.

The Inner Inadequacies: Sin/Corruption, Dualistic Worldview, Alien Theology

Certainly, we don't fully appreciate the power of sin and the devil, but Christ has won the victory and I'm not sure how helpful the section on "A dualistic worldview" is without further explanation. I agree that individualism and dualism (spirit vs matter) lead to a horrible deformation of Christian faith, thought, and life. In my view, Platonic dualism and European Enlightenment, rationalism and individualism are the real culprits. I think that the Jewish tradition and the Aristotelian philosophical tradition are more promising resources.

But if we return to the temptations faced by our Lord and by us today, the answer is not to be found rummaging around among the philosophers and theologians but rather in knowing Scripture (as Jesus quoted to the Tempter) and being secure in one's identity as a beloved son or daughter of God. Our problem today is that we do not know Scripture and we do not draw our identity from God. Christians do not know the Decalogue, they do not know the Proverbs, the Sermon on the Mount, Romans 12–13, etc. Scripture is, to most Christians, a random collection of therapeutic sayings with no context. Christians in business often have no clue about Jesus' teachings on money, property and wealth. Christians in law have no clue what Scripture teaches about law and justice.

Moreover, Christians tend to draw their identity more from their social, national or regional groupings than from the transnational, transhistorical, kingdom of God, where our real citizenship lies. We habitually *yield* to authority when we should always *question* authority as the Berean saints did. Do not be conformed to this world. Any of it. In the world but not of the world. Thy will be done on earth — not the will of the earth be done. We Christians so lack this sense of our identity in Christ and his kingdom. Of course our true identity brings with it a community — rather than individualistic — ethics, an ethics of service instead of lordship, reconciliation instead of conflict, stewardship instead of consumption, etc.

Yes, all Western deformations of Christian theology and ethics must be rejected without hesitation. Dualism must be rejected for the heresy that it is.

Developing a Theology of Social Engagement

Fundamental Principles

My hierarchy of fundamental principles for constructing an ethics or a theology of social engagement are: (a) centred on Jesus Christ; (b) guided by Scripture; (c) informed by the church; and (d) practised in the world (explained in my book *Doing Right: Practicing Ethical Principles*). This is the path by which I would develop such a theology or ethics.

It has built-in guards against becoming an apology for one culture or another and yet it must be "walked" in a specific culture or it is not complete.

An Incarnational Model

I don't think it helps to go back to Ernst Troeltsch, Reinhold Niebuhr, or Robert Webber. They provide "ideal types" which emerged in historical epochs different from our own; historically interesting but not practically helpful for the people we are trying to help. I'd urge you to plunge directly into the development of your Incarnational model: centred on Jesus Christ.

One process observation: an ethics of principles, decision, and action really needs to be built on an ethics of character and community. You must be born again — not just be given a better set of principles. New character, new community: this ethics of virtue is the only foundation on which an ethics of principles will have any chance of success.

Application: Corruption

This careful essay on bribery and corruption makes a lot of sense to me. We need to get away from legalism and formalism and ask "what is the point here?" What are the values we are trying to protect? Corruption of justice and fairness? Unloading needed medical supplies off of a boat? Pleasing the WTO? What are the values we see in our Lord? In the rest of Scripture? How does the body of Christ see it here and now? And in other eras and locations? How can we be more far-sighted, seeing problems before they get to us so we can act creatively and faithfully while situations are still fluid? How can we ensure that our decisions are collaborative and accompanied by prayerful discernment? Can we live more transparent lives, ready to acknowledge and take responsibility for the discernment and action we have embraced? Can we as Christians "salt" the marketplace as an inexhaustible source of creative, redemptive ideas and options? Will we learn to be bold leaders and humbler servants at the same time, like our Lord?

Endnotes

1. I would recommend *Bad Samaritans* by Ha-Joon Chang as an important counterpoint to current Western notions of ethical globalisation and successful development.

2. My own understanding of Christian ethics is given in two books: *Becoming Good: Building Moral Character* (InterVarsity, 2000) and *Doing Right: Practicing Ethical Principles* (InterVarsity, 2004). My understanding of business ethics for a global, diverse marketplace is given in *It's About Excellence: Building Ethically Healthy Organizations* (Provo, UT: Executive Excellence Publishing, 2008). I publish a free, monthly "EthixBizine" from my website: www.ethixbiz.com.

Chapter 7

Response *by* Pijar Kurniawan

Alumnus, Indonesian State College of Accountancy, Jakarta
Directorate General of Customs and Excise, Ministry of Finance, Indonesia

"Treasure, throne, woman" is a popular phrase in Indonesia. These three things can easily distract us, especially Christians, from the Holy Trinity of "God the Father, Christ the Son, and the Holy Spirit". Bishop Hwa Yung in his book *Bribery and Corruption: Biblical Reflections and Case Studies for the Marketplace in Asia*, uses another phrase, "money, sex and power", likewise alerting the reader to the three main things that affect us every day. These pressures, as described in Chapter 1, often cause Christians to fail in fulfilling the will of our Creator. Coupled with our human inadequacy to cope with such pressures, it becomes more apparent why it is difficult to be unaffected (directly or indirectly) by bribery and corruption.

As someone who works in a field of governance which incidentally has the stigma of being a 'swamp' for bribery and corruption, I find that this book is very relevant for those interested in the local culture and dynamics of the church in Asia. Bribery is already entrenched in the smallest unit of community, the family. In fact, I argued with my parents when they gave me a driver's license without my having to sit for any test. The relational and familial culture often perceives unsolicited gifts as a blessing, and to reject a gift would mean being ungrateful.

The abundance of imported Christian literature in bookstores does not necessarily make the struggle of Christians in Indonesia easier to bear. A small gap appears in books from Western countries. This has been noticed by Bishop Hwa Yung, and his book, rooted in Asian culture, fills this need. In view of Asian habits such as *guanxi* in China and close kinship ties among Asians, readers are compelled to re-examine the ethical and moral principles of Christianity in order to stay grounded and make decisions without selfish compromises, knowing that we are answerable to God.

The other strength of this book lies in its concept. Instead of an immediate answer (or judgement) on the struggles of bribery and corruption, theological considerations are presented to marketplace practitioners dealing with situations that relate directly or indirectly with corruption. The author examines the thoughts and feelings of his readers, and helps us understand that bribery and corruption in Asia is really all around us. We need great energy to fight them with wisdom such as that found in the book of Proverbs.

Several principles, alternatives and practical guidelines are presented vividly in this book. It would have been nice if the key points were worded as catchphrases that can be easily remembered and applied. Besides that, some footnotes are full of important information and should be part of the text, lest some readers skip them. Another concern is the frequent use of the word 'no' and 'not'. Part 1 alone has 19 instances of 'no' in Chapter 1, 23 in Chapter 2 and 66 in Chapter 3. The entire book is filled with 215 'no's and 15 'not's. This lends a negative tone throughout. Although Bishop Hwa Yung writes in the Introduction that he hopes to motivate readers to actively and optimistically respond to bribery and corruption, the book seems to confirm that what readers have experienced is in line with the contents of the book and what the Bible says about the situation.

The book is thoughtfully accompanied by theological responses (part 2) and case studies (part 3). This makes the reader feel less alone in struggling to combat bribery and corruption at work. However, it would be more complete if Bishop Hwa Yung also commented on the legal aspect of the issues at hand. The law, after all, is a control element when the level of ethics and morals is low.

I am sure this book will bring inspiration and hope to the reader. I was inspired by what Bishop Hwa Yung told his students: "Do not do a very different ugliness by doing good." May we be ambassadors of God's Kingdom, actively bringing good to the marketplace where we are.

Chapter 8

Response *by* Yulius Tandyanto

Bahasa Indonesia translator of *Bribery and Corruption*
Graduate Student, Driyarkara College of Philosophy, Jakarta

For me, Hwa Yung presents a theology that is bold, practical, and truly intertwined with the lives of Christians in Asia. In Eastern cultures, bribery and petty corruption are commonplace in business practices and bureaucracy. It is as if acts of bribery and corruption have been an undisputed part of oriental traditions. Like lubricating oil that is needed to smooth rigid and hard wheels, such is the function of a bribe for the wheels of bureaucracy.

Moreover, Hwa's boldness in presenting such an Asian theology is because of his courage to dismantle the dualistic understanding that is so entrenched among many Christians. Take these for example: body and soul, world and heaven, mortal and eternal. Too often, we give negative ratings to the first aspect (the body, the world and the mortal). As a result, attempts to become salt and light in the world are not taken seriously and intentionally. After all, we think that eternal life has nothing to do with things that are of this world.

Based on this popular understanding, Hwa shows that theology needs to be rooted in culture. As Christ incarnate came into the world, so the theology of incarnation has the power to change a damaged order. Of course, expected changes do not necessarily lead to desired results. Instead, we will encounter dilemmas, difficulties and even failure thanks to efforts to block such improvements. In such situations, Hwa exhorts us to appreciate each process and work in accordance with our abilities and callings.

All this to say: Hwa's book is a brave book, practical, and sincerely invites every Christian to be involved in their work lives.

SECTION 3 *CASE STUDIES*

Chapter 9

Case Study *by* Sherman Lam

An Asian marketplace practitioner

When I first received the invitation to respond to Bishop Rev. Hwa Yung's paper, I had two competing thoughts. On the one hand, I found it daunting to think about how I could add value — intellectually, biblically and theologically — to his piece. On the other hand, I was hesitant to pass up this valuable opportunity to be of service to my brothers and sisters in Asia. After struggling for a few days, I decided to accept the challenge and have tried, from a practitioner's perspective, to share three real-life cases regarding the application of the transformation principle in the marketplace. Two of the three cases happened to people I know and trust. The third case is a personal encounter. Two took place in China and one in Vietnam.

Case 1

The first case happened to A, my ex-colleague in a multinational energy company, some 15 years ago. A was then the head of the company's gas business in Greater China and also a new Christian who was fervently preaching the Gospel to his colleagues. Like most multinational corporations, the company had issued clear guidelines on handling ethical issues when doing business in developing countries like China. However, each business unit head, including A, was under pressure to reach annual sales and profit targets. A was working hard to tap the gas trading market in China and had come to a point where a sales and purchase agreement was about to be finalised. The only thing left was for the officer in charge of the state-owned gas company to sign the agreement. At this time the officer revealed his personal agenda and requested a "consultancy fee" of US$5 per ton to be paid to his personal account in Hong Kong. Familiar with this game, A did not pay the "consultancy fee" himself but asked his staff to do it. The deal was concluded.

Based on Bishop Rev. Hwa Yung's classification, this case should be categorised as "passive acceptance" of corruption rather than "active corruption" and A would fit the "identificational model". Though he was involuntarily involved in the bribe, A did make the final decision and was morally wrong — but I would argue that his act was understandable. Given his then-level of spiritual maturity, A lacked the required training, knowledge and awareness to address such an ethical challenge in a mature, biblical way and hence relied on his usual ways of doing business.

Case 2

The second case was encountered by B, one of my best Christian friends who was based in Singapore. B was a brilliant engineer and had been promoted to head a sales team in a telecommunication engineering company. Six years ago, when the Technology, Media and Telecoms (TMT) bubble burst, B's company faced great financial difficulty and desperately needed to expand into neighbouring countries like Vietnam. B was tasked to bid for a telecommunication network project in Hanoi and was told by his boss that if B failed, he would be sacked together with the other members of his team. When he was bidding for the project, the officer-in-charge in the Vietnamese company demanded a consultancy fee of 20 percent to be paid to the overseas account of a designated consultancy firm that had no involvement in the project. That officer warned B that if he did not do this, he would not have any chance of winning the contract.

> **"But as a team leader he felt a strong obligation to look after the interests of his team members."**

Having been a committed Christian for a long time, B was committed to living a life with high moral standards. Now, for the first time, B was confronted with a major ethical problem. He tried to seek help from his boss but received a cold shoulder. He did think of seeking support and guidance from his pastor and other fellow Christians in Singapore, but finally decided not to do so as most of them functioned with a "dualistic world-view" and "lifeboat ethics", in the terms of Bishop Hwa Yung. His staff pleaded with him to compromise, as they desperately needed their jobs to support their families amidst the economic downturn.

This put B in a dilemma — if he only considered his own convictions, he would choose not to bribe and just quit.

But as a team leader he felt a strong obligation to look after the interests of his team members. In the Chinese/Asian working culture, B was a "big brother" to his staff. In fact, he loved them. After praying, wrestling and weeping before the Lord, B chose to pay the consultancy fee, but on the condition that the related consultancy company be dissolved and its overseas account closed down after the deal was completed. As a result, he helped his company win the contract and his team members kept their jobs. As for B, to hold himself accountable for what he had done, he resigned after everything had been settled.

This case should also be classified as "passive acceptance" of corruption and would be in line with Hwa Yung's "incarnational model". It was a tragic choice. What B did was wrong but, I would argue, acceptable and perhaps wise. He compromised, not for his own benefit, but for the desperate needs of his staff.

After an immense inner struggle, B chose relationships over principle. He "sinned boldly" but in a confessional spirit. This case highlights the following questions that Asian Christians need to explore further:

(a) Should we make ethical decisions based on rules (deontological), results (teleological), relationships (love) or a combination of the three? How do we balance the three given the merits of different specific situations?

(b) How should we view compromise? Can we accept a principled compromise in an extreme situation? Can we even see that sometimes compromise can be a Christian response?

(c) If a moral man commits an immoral act for a noble cause, can we still regard him as "moral"? Can "doing" be separate from "being" in an extreme situation?

Answering the above questions is difficult, and not helped by the fact that the prevailing theology adopted by most Asian churches is an import from the West and is, in substance, either fundamentalist or, (its variant) charismatic. Our ethical thinking leans towards either legalistic rigidity or simplistic naivety and triumphalism.

Case 3

The last case is a personal story. Four years ago, when I was in between jobs, I ran a one-man company that provided advisory services on incubations. Knowing my background in energy and power industries, a client approached me to help him source a contractor to construct a small hydro-electric power station in an inland county of China. The station would be owned and operated under a joint venture between my client and the county government. It was agreed that the former was responsible for the construction and the latter would provide the necessary land and labour.

The crux of the issue was determining the value of each party's contribution. My client demanded that the construction contractor must be willing to mark the contract at a face value of RMB200M, but with a kickback of RMB100M to him. In other words, in the books of the joint venture, the construction cost would be RMB200M, although my client would only pay RMB100M. In return, I would receive HK$1M as a middleman's fee. It sounded easy and attractive. I promised my client to source the contractor for him.

After meeting my client, I found myself confronting a major conflict between my mind and my heart. My mind kept thinking about how, as a middleman, I could pretend not to know the actual terms between my client and the contractor, and hence could justify that my hands were not dirty. But deep in my heart, I felt extremely uncomfortable with the deal.

Shortly afterwards, I met up with a group of Christians who were discussing how they could advance the marketplace ministry in Hong Kong. I shared my struggle with them. They did not judge me but, gently, they said, "Sherman, you know the answer." They were right. I knew the answer. Thanks to the Lord's wake-up call through these brothers, I turned down my client's offer.

This case goes beyond corruption. It includes fraud, cheating, kickbacks, forensic accounting, etc., and would demand a "separational model" response. As Bishop Rev. Hwa Yung rightly pointed out, Christians tend to over-estimate their inner spiritual strength. Frankly, I admit that I almost fell into this snare because of greed and my obsession with success. In facing external pressures such as the temptations of money, sex and power, we need to recognise our inner inadequacies and seek support from fellow Christians. I was lucky to have a fellowship of mature marketplace practitioners who gave me spiritual and professional advice. However, I wonder whether this type of fellowship is common or rare in Asia? What kind of support, resources and training are available for the many

Asian Christians who struggle with ethical decisions in the marketplace?

Conclusion

Other than the above three cases, I would like to echo Bishop Rev. Hwa Yung's call in Guideline 5: We must never lose sight of the transformation principle that is built on the Christian's calling to be "salt" and "light". Transformation can hardly be effected on the individual level alone. It needs the influence of corporations and governments.

I once served in a Hong Kong power company whose management was making consistent and persistent efforts to upgrade its corporate governance and ethical standards. The company devised a Code of Conduct that clearly laid down the company's stands on corruption, bribery, fraud, insider trading, confidentiality, privacy, non-compliance with statutory and regulatory requirements, etc. In order to ensure that the company's requirements were understood by the staff, the management periodically organised training programmes for employees and required mid-to-senior-level staff to declare, on an annual basis, whether they had complied with the company's Code of Conduct.

> **"...we need to recognise our inner inadequacies and seek support from fellow Christians."**

As a result, the company successfully cultivated a culture of doing business ethically, not only in Hong Kong and Australia, but also in the Chinese mainland, Taiwan, Thailand, and India. I believe Christian businessmen and executives can bring about moral transformation through the influence of corporations and businesses.

Christians in public service too should do their part. Previously, corruption and bribery were endemic in Hong Kong. "Tea money", "black money", "hell money" — bribes by various names — were very familiar to Hong Kong people. But since the inception of the Independent Commission Against Corruption in 1974, anti-corruption reform has seen dramatic progress through law enforcement, prevention and community education. As a result, Hong Kong has now become one of the most corruption-free places in the world.

However, I am aware that each country has its own history and baggage. The Malaysian Church is a different battle-field. May the Lord strengthen our Malaysian brothers and sisters to fight the good fight for Him! Amen.

Chapter 10

Case Study *by* Dr H

An Asian healthcare practitioner

Dr H is a shareholder and director of a company that specialises in healthcare technology. He has handled many government contracts. Once, the company clinched a multi-million-dollar project from the government to advise, evaluate, project-manage and commission the implementation of a Hospital Information System in a number of public hospitals.

The government had awarded the contract to the company because of its expertise, and part of the scope of the project was to advise the government on the procurement of multi-million dollars' worth of healthcare technology. It was expected that Dr H would use his technical expertise to safeguard the government's interest and investment through a fair, transparent and objective procurement process. Despite knowing that corruptive practices were taking place in the industry, Dr H attempted to make a difference by carrying out the work objectively.

In the process of doing an audit of the hospitals, Dr H discovered that contracts given to companies did not go through an open tender procedure. The companies were given "letters of intent" on the basis of political patronage and there were no proper specifications and submission processes. Product prices were also grossly inflated. Subsequently, he learnt that the government machinery had many leakages of funds, and that most of the companies that had clinched major contracts had their respective political patrons who benefited from the business transactions.

Dr H believed that if this corrupt practice were to be left unchecked, the resulting "inefficiency" would threaten the well-being of the public healthcare system which was already struggling with escalating costs. However, he said it seemed almost futile to try to stop these leakages from taking place as the corrupt practices were widespread among government officials and even some hospital staff. He added that, while some practices were clearly corrupt in nature, there were many other practices that fell within "grey areas", as these could be seen as goodwill gestures. These "grey" areas included the giving of gifts to certain parties that had influential powers within the government machinery.

While Dr H had avoided such practices, they were considered a norm and a courteous gesture to high-ranking officials. Such gifts could range from the latest handphones, to laptop computers, to overseas holidays for the officials' families, to "kickbacks" based on a percentage of the contract value, depending on the rank of the official, as well as his or her influence in recommending a company to clinch the project.

Dr H said that he had also been approached by "political lobbyists" who claimed that they represented the "interests" of some politicians and that they could provide assistance in procuring contracts (some multi-million-dollar contracts can be secured even without open tenders). However, if a company refused to condone such practices, he said it would face barriers in sealing deals, as there would be parties that could easily sabotage the company's chances of securing the contract.

Dr H found himself "between a rock and a hard place". His company was already facing liquidity problems as it had yet to receive payments from the government. It was also very difficult to try to uphold integrity in the prevailing environment as the company might be questioned for doing so. He said the company had even been subjected to various criticisms and allegations that the integrity and honesty portrayed by Dr H and his subordinates were false.

To make matters worse, Dr H also faced criticism from the company's shareholders, as not all of them shared his convictions about upholding integrity at the workplace. He said that he, however, was not worried about folding up the company, if that became necessary, as he had conducted the businesses of the company with the best possible practices and a clear conscience. However, he faced the dilemma of having to retrench his employees who had been loyal to the company.

Dr H said that he has yet to meet a fellow Christian in this industry and therefore had never had the opportunity to discuss issues pertaining to bribery and corruption in the healthcare industry from a Christian perspective. However, he took comfort in being able to share the Gospel with his employees under such circumstances, as they were intrigued by Dr H's perseverance in not giving in to bribery and other corrupt practices.

Chapter 11

Case Study *by* Mr C

A businessman in the Asian construction industry

Applying the "Incarnational Model" in practice: The Problem of Corruption

The "Alternative 1 Option", to opt for jobs in certain "safe" sectors, is quite difficult for people in the construction industry, one which has been aptly described as "a jungle of concrete and steel".

In some countries in Asia, corruption in the government sector is, in fact, the major contributory factor to corruption in the private sector. Politics and business are closely linked and the civil service is largely controlled and influenced by politicians. Once corruption starts from the highest levels of the political and civil service hierarchy, it permeates down to the lowest level, to the office clerk who ensures that your file is not left at the bottom of the pile.

During the last major recession in 1998, many development projects in Asia were stopped and even government contracts were scarce. In one of the Asian countries, the government development policy then was to concentrate on low-cost housing projects with a target selling price of US$13,500 per unit. Due to limited suitable land in the selected area, most of the projects had to be on disused mining land where the costs of building the foundations would be high.

> "Once corruption starts from the highest levels of the political and civil service hierarchy, it permeates down to the lowest levels..."

My company managed to propose an alternative, technically equivalent foundation system which was much cheaper and at a development cost that would allow the selling price of the unit to remain at US$13,500. We engaged a reputable consultant to support our alternative design and made a presentation to the government authority. Subsequently, several unofficial meetings were arranged where "approval fees" could be negotiated and agreed upon before formal approval could be given.

We were in a dilemma as the projects were crucial for turning around our company which had hardly secured any projects for more than a year. There were financial commitments to the banks, the monthly operating expenses and staff salaries. As subcontractor to the main contractor, we therefore had to increase our quoted cost in order to take care of the "approval fees" and other political contributions that were mainly handled by the main contractors.

The above experience is just an example of the dilemma we face in trying to be "in the world" and yet "not of the world". It is also an example of "passive acceptance" of corruption when dealing with government authorities. However, we also have developers in the private sector who are ethical and professional. They are transparent and emphasise to us verbally (and some even in writing) that their organisations do not tolerate any form of corruption.

This extends to not accepting any form of gifts, *ang pows* (red packets containing cash gifts) or entertainment for their staff or consultants. We truly hope and look forward to the day when this excellent ethical culture can permeate the whole of the building industry.

We know it is possible because there are indeed countries in Asia where the business environment, be it in the government or private sector, is professional, clean and transparent. There is absolutely no expectation from any party for any form of "extra payment" beyond the terms and conditions of the contracts. Why are the situations so different in these countries?

I can only conclude that in some countries, a conscious decision was made to accept "zero tolerance" of any form of corruption at all levels of the government — both in policy and in action. All construction contracts in the government and private sectors are awarded based on their merits and on the most competitive pricing.

Ethics in Business

I would like to also emphasise the need for Christian ethics in business which may not be directly related to corruption, but which have significant impact on the parties we deal with. Bishop Hwa Yung's opening Bible quote, "Let your light so shine before men that they may see your good works and glorify your Father who is in heaven", is relevant for Christian businessmen to shine in our good works.

1. Staff welfare

As Christian business employers, we should always ensure that staff salaries are paid promptly before month's end or, at the latest, by the first week of the following month. Sometimes, however, there may be crisis situations when drastic measures are called for to ensure the survival of the company. Even then, we should try our best as employers to do right by our employees. We encountered this during the 1998 financial downturn.

When we had to carry out staff retrenchments, we gave them sufficient notice so that they were able to secure new jobs before leaving. Salary reviews/reductions were carried out on a graduated scale from the directors' level (70%) to the managers' level (10-20%). Staff earning salaries below US$600.00 were not affected as we felt this was the minimum they could survive on.

These were painful and tough decisions that needed to be taken, but this was done holding in tension the priority of staff welfare and the company's survival.

2. Suppliers /subcontractors

While recognising that we should endeavour to make prompt payments, the existing business environment is often not conducive to this. Cash flow, therefore, can become a challenge and involve a tough balancing exercise each month. Most of us are therefore quite used to delayed payments. However, the real challenge comes during a financial/economic crisis when many companies take the opportunity to delay payments unnecessarily. In the building industry, once the developer defaults on payment, the chain reaction will be passed down all the way to the staff and workers.

During the 1998 crisis, we had debtors owing us up to US$3 Million and creditors needing to be paid up to US$2 Million. It took us almost five years to manage to collect sufficient funds to settle what we owed either in cash or in other form of assets. Several companies merely took the easier route of winding up and defaulting on all payments.

3. *Housing development*

We often read in the news of home buyers who, after partial or almost full payment of the price for their purchased units, are faced with delayed or abandoned projects. Completed units are also either of poor quality or filled with defects. Christian developers need to carefully consider the feasibility of their projects before launching them, as any failure would affect and may even destroy the life savings of many people.

I have several Christian friends in the housing development business who are ethical and responsible, and therefore bear good testimony to their beliefs. However, there was a company started by a Christian in the early 1990s that successfully developed and sold all the units in one of its projects, with good profits. The company was subsequently taken over by another group which mismanaged the company. Till this day, the completed project (15 years later) has yet to receive a full CF (Certificate of Fitness) because the development charges have not been paid to the land office. The purchasers found that the value of their properties had depreciated well below market value and even below the original purchase price. Many of them found themselves in a fix because banks are not prepared to finance loans for units that do not have a full CF.

On hindsight, the Christian shareholders should have ensured that all payments had been fully settled and proper CFs obtained before the new shareholders took over the management of the company. We have a moral responsibility to ensure that as much of the related parties' welfare is fully taken care of before we exit from our business ventures.

Although the above example may not be related to corruption, it is an example of Christian ethics in business which can be more damaging directly to innocent people if we are not careful.

In conclusion, Bishop Hwa Yung's paper provides us a good biblical and realistic basis to think through the Christian ethical issues that confront us. My journey in the business world has been tough and challenging. Looking back, it is only by God's grace that I have been able to survive. Through the years, the journey has been at times lonely as we have found it difficult to share these issues at the church level. As Bishop Hwa Yung has rightly pointed out, the

Rapids, MI: Baker, 1989.

Perkin, Harold. *The Origins of Modern English Society (1780–1880)*. 2nd ed. Oxford, UK: Routledge, 2002.

Pollock, John. *Wilberforce*. Berkhamsted, UK: Lion, 1977.

Tomkins, Stephen. *The Clapham Sect: How Wilberforce's Circle Transformed Britain*. Oxford, UK: Lion Hudson, 2010.

Webber, Robert E. *The Secular Saint: The Role of the Christian in the Secular World*. Grand Rapids, MI: Zondervan, 1979.

Wraith, Ronald, and Edgar Simpkins. *Corruption in Developing Countries*. London, UK: George Allen & Unwin, 1963.

Conclusion

Stott, John R. W. *Involvement: Being a responsible Christian in a non-Christian society*. Ney York, NY: F. H. Revell Company, 1985.

Chapter 4

Cosden, Darrell. *The Heavenly Good of Earthly Work*. Peabody, MA: Hendrickson Publishers, 2006.

Erisman, Albert M. "Case Studies in Business Ethics." Seminar at Urbana 2006, the InterVarsity Christian Fellowship Missions Conference, St. Louis, MO., December 30, 2006.

Richter, Frank Jurgen and Pamela C.M. Mar. *Asia's New Crisis: Renewal Through Total Ethical Management*. Singapore: John Wiley and Sons (Asia), 2004.

Stevens, R. Paul. "A Contextualized Theology of Work for Asia: an expanded summary deriving from discussions during the Asian consultation on Marketplace Theology." Lecture notes, delivered in Manila, sponsored by the Bakke Graduate University, November 28–30, 2007.

Wright, N.T. *Surprised by Hope: Rethinking Heaven, the Resurrection, and the Mission of the Church*. New York, NY: HarperCollins, 2008.

CHAPTER 5

Noonan, John T., Jr. "Bribery". In *A New Dictionary of Christian Ethics*, eds. John Macquarrie and James Childress. Philadelphia, PA: Westminster Press, 1986, 65f.

CHAPTER 6

Chang, Ha-Joon. *Bad Samaritans: The Myth of Free Trade and the Secret History of Capitalism*. New York, NY: Bloomsbury Press, 2008.

Gill, David W. *Becoming Good: Building Moral Character*. Downers Grove, IL: InterVarsity Press, 2000.

—, *Doing Right: Practicing Ethical Principles*. Downers Grove, IL: InterVarsity Press, 2004.

—, *It's About Excellence: Building Ethically Healthy Organizations*. Provo, UT: Executive Excellence Publishing, 2008.

Hwa Yung was the bishop of the Methodist Church in Malaysia from 2004–2012. During his ministry he was a pastor and seminary lecturer. He has served as the Principal of Malaysia Theological Seminary (STM) and the Director of the Centre for the Study of Christianity in Asia, Trinity Theological College, Singapore. He has also served on the Council of the Oxford Centre for Mission Studies and the Lausanne International Board. Currently, he is the Honorary President of IFES (2011–2019).

GRACEWORKS

Graceworks is a publishing and training consultancy based in Singapore, dedicated to promoting spiritual friendship in church and society, and seeing lives transformed through books that present truth for life.

Our publications can be found on our online store, *www.graceworks.com.sg/store*. Paperbacks are also available on Book Depository and Amazon. eBooks on Kindle, iBooks and Kobo. You can contact us at *enquiries@graceworks.com.sg*, or follow us on Facebook (@GraceworksSG) and Instagram (graceworkssg).